Original title:
The Charm of Every Day

Copyright © 2025 Creative Arts Management OÜ
All rights reserved.

Author: Ethan Prescott
ISBN HARDBACK: 978-1-80586-086-0
ISBN PAPERBACK: 978-1-80586-558-2

Windows to Everyday Wonder

When the toast pops up, I cheer,
A dance with crumbs, never fear.
Socks mismatched, what a delight,
Laughter echoes through the night.

A cat that leaps, then misses all,
Bouncing off the kitchen wall.
A plant that whispers silly things,
Leaves of laughter, joy it brings.

Coffee spills, a tiny lake,
Stirring chaos with each shake.
Chasing sunbeams like a fool,
Every day, a new rule.

A doorbell rings with random chimes,
Postman's here with bags of rhymes.
In the mundane, joy we find,
Every moment, light and kind.

Echoes of Footsteps in Time

Sneakers squeak on kitchen floors,
Dancing clumsily, laughter roars.
The dog joins in, a furry muse,
Chasing shadows, endless snooze.

Sipping tea like royalty,
Spilling some, oh what a spree!
Each drop tells a story sweet,
Joyful chaos, life's heartbeat.

The thermostat's a sneaky foe,
Too cold, too hot, now let it go.
Socks in the fridge? Who could tell?
Every day feels like a spell.

As daytime wanes and stars peek through,
I toast to oddities, and it's true,
In moments mundane, we find the fun,
Dancing life's dance, we've just begun.

Ordinary Wonders Unveiled

In the morning, socks mismatched,
A coffee cup with a silly scratch.
Butterflies in my toast today,
What a joyous start to play!

The cat in the window, oh so grand,
Chasing shadows with a flick of his hand.
Birds gossiping high up in trees,
Nature laughing in the cool morning breeze.

Traces of Tranquility

The clock ticks loudly, yet feels so slow,
A dance of dust in the evening glow.
Neighbors argue over a stray cat,
Meanwhile, I'm stuck wearing a hat!

Lost in chores, yet I see the light,
A mismatched sock, what a funny sight!
The TV buzzes with old reruns,
While I chuckle at my silly puns.

The Rhythm of Daily Life

Breakfast plans that all went wrong,
Jam spilled like a comical song.
Grocery lists, a wild affair,
End up buying cupcakes, I swear!

Old shoes squeaking, they groan and moan,
Each step forward now feels like a groan.
Yet laughter bubbles, bright and clear,
Even in chaos, joy appears!

Lullabies of the Living

Naps interrupted by loud sneezes,
Cuddly pets have all the breezes.
The laundry dances, a circus show,
While I just watch, saying, 'Oh no!'

Dinner's a riddle, a food puzzle game,
Burnt the bread, but who's really to blame?
Under the stars, I hear crickets sing,
In this daily chaos, oh, what joy it brings!

Breath of Life's Little Moments

A sock on the floor, it has great reviews,
It whispers sweet secrets, and other odd clues.
A cat in a box is the king of his realm,
While we sip our coffee, he takes on the helm.

The toast that pops up, like it's ready to play,
Looks like a hot rocket on a thrilling parade.
Each crumb that we drop turns into a race,
As ants take a lane for their little food chase.

Gifts Wrapped in Familiarity

The morning sun dances on windowpanes bright,
As mismatched socks giggle in a joyful delight.
A rogue rubber band takes an unexpected flight,
While the toaster sings tunes that tickle our sight.

Each spilled cup of cereal brings laughter galore,
With milk fountains leaping, who could ask for more?
The laundry pile whispers tales from the floor,
While dust bunnies scheme to settle the score.

Starlight in the Commonplace

A spoon's doing ballet, a fork in the fray,
While the fridge hums a tune, oh what a display!
The dog on the mat dreams of chasing his tail,
And we giggle at cats who invent their own tale.

The light switch flickers like it's playing a game,
As shadows stampede, but none get the fame.
The rug squeaks in laughter, all silent it seems,
And we've lost every match against our own dreams.

Enchantment Beneath the Ordinary

The doorbell's a jester, it jumps and it rings,
While dust motes boogie like they're born to be kings.
The garden gnome winks with a mischievous glare,
As he plots his escape with the neighbor's old chair.

The rain on the window draws pictures, it seems,
A world that can giggle inside of our dreams.
Each sigh of the kettle, each clank of a pot,
Turns breakfast to circus, connecting the dots.

Whispers of Dawn

Sunbeam tickles my sleepy face,
Coffee spills at a frantic pace,
Sock puppets dance, a funny sight,
Morning giggles take their flight.

Birds chatter like they're in a play,
Toast pops up, in a funny way,
Cats plot mischief, oh what a sight,
Dancing shadows in morning light.

Radiance in Routine

Breakfast choices make me chuckle,
Cereal spills, oh what a shuffle!
Matching socks is a daily quest,
Laundry monsters never rest.

Juggling keys, I make a dive,
Trip over shoes, I barely survive,
Hum a tune, and dance with flair,
Who knew chaos could be so rare?

Moments in the Mundane

Chasing down the wanderlust dog,
He found a fence post, like a log,
Grocery lists become a race,
Check my phone, lost in space.

Neighbors wave, their expressions bright,
Mowing lawns in a silly fight,
Autumn leaves play tag on the ground,
Life's little quirks are all around.

Echoes of Ordinary Splendor

Lunch breaks filled with laughter loud,
Pasta flings like a dynamo crowd,
Muffins dance and tease my plate,
Every joke feels very great.

Evening falls, we gather round,
With board games, joy can be found,
Who knew life could be so light?
In every moment, giggles ignite.

Serenity in Simplicity

A sock's lone journey, lost with flair,
A dance with dust bunnies in the air.
The kettle whistles a high-pitched song,
As coffee spills on the desk all along.

The cat plays king on a throne of chairs,
While I trip over forgotten wares.
Sunshine spills in through a window crack,
But I'm still searching for my missing snack.

The Grace of Unseen Hours

Timing is key when the toast pops up,
But a jammed lid ruins my tea cup.
Time ticks by in jumps and skips,
As I chase after my runaway chips.

A pencil rolls off, no sound to greet,
I trip on air, my own two feet.
Each day's a joke, a playful tease,
What's left of order blows with the breeze.

Treasures in Tedium

Sorting through socks, a mundane feat,
Each one a story, a memory sweet.
A puzzle piece hides beneath the couch,
Whispering secrets like a mischievous slouch.

Dust gathers thick like the best of friends,
Each speck a legend that never ends.
Life's little quirks, oh how they shine,
My clumsy dance with breakfast divine.

Beauty in the Banal

A wilted plant, yet it stands so proud,
Beneath the weight of a raincloud.
My sandwich sighs with existential dread,
But I still devour it, crumbs on the bed.

A scuff on the shoe tells a wild tale,
Of puddles jumped and a gusty gale.
The fridge hums soft in the evening glow,
While leftovers plot a culinary show.

Glances of Glistening Moments

In the morning sun, I trip and fall,
My coffee spills, I laugh through it all.
Butterflies dance, as they mock me so,
I blink twice fast, while they put on a show.

A squirrel steals my bagel, grinning with pride,
I chase after it, my dignity slides.
The whole park giggles at my clumsy feet,
Yet I find pure joy in this silly defeat.

Footprints in Familiar Sand

Waves crash and splash, my toes in a curl,
I trip on a shell, give a wild twirl.
The seagulls squawk, as if they approve,
My dance is absurd, but I've got the groove.

The sun shines bright, a hot poker game,
With melting ice cream, it's all kind of lame.
But laughter erupts with a scoff and a grin,
Each silly moment makes me feel like a win.

Nuances of the Now

A cat on a roof, what a sight to behold,
It struts like a king, so brazen, so bold.
I wave at the neighbors, who stare in surprise,
A circus of nonsense unfolds before eyes.

The neighbor's dog barks, a confused little roar,
While I fumble and trip on the squeaking front door.
Laughter bursts forth like bubbles in soda,
And life seems a joke that never grows older.

Whisking Away the Ordinary

In the kitchen chaos, I whisk and I twirl,
Batter on my nose, oh what a mishmash swirl!
The omelette flips, but ends up as goo,
I laugh at my chef skills, all out of view.

The clock ticks away as I dance with the broom,
Cleaning with flair, giving dust bunnies doom.
Every laugh echoes, as I trip on my feet,
In this comedy show, every moment's a treat.

Dances in Fleeting Glances

In coffee cups, dreams swirl around,
A giggle escapes, and joy is found.
Socks that don't match, oh what a sight,
Tripping on laughter, it feels so right.

A cat steals my chair, lays down with flair,
While I wander off, unaware of where.
Banana peels slide, a slip and a slide,
We tumble and roll, joy can't be denied.

Shadows and Sunbeams

A squirrel steals snacks, oh what a thief,
He prances and dances, brings me such grief.
Sunbeams slide in, in warms and in glows,
While shadows stretch out like a child's big toes.

A puddle reflects a dapper old frog,
He croaks out a tune, a real party bog.
Sidewalk chalk art, the colors collide,
Who knew masterpieces could happen outside?

Unfolding the Unremarkable

A toast with toast, that burns on the edge,
I laugh at the crumbs that cling to the ledge.
Each book on the shelf whispers tales so clear,
Of giants and goblins, they're all waiting here.

A pigeon struts by in a hat made of fluff,
He's living his best life, oh isn't that tough?
A missing left shoe brings giggles aloud,
In a world where mismatches form quite a crowd.

Mosaic of Daily Treasures

A keychain's a compass that points to my heart,
It's lost, but the search is a fine work of art.
Bubbles in baths create castles galore,
While rubber ducks host a royal encore.

The mailman's a dancer, so sprightly and spry,
Delivering letters while winking an eye.
Scraps from my lunch, become gourmet dreams,
Every day's menu is rich, or so it seems.

Emblems of Everyday Enchantment

Some socks always dance, in a merry pair,
While breakfast burns, filling the kitchen air.
The cat steals my seat, with a royal remark,
Yet she purrs like a queen, in the glow of the dark.

The mailman jogs, with letters galore,
Mails dreams and rumors, that I can't ignore.
The plants also gossip, with leaves in a spin,
While I sip my coffee, inviting a grin.

A spoon drops 'cause it's eager to groove,
While I try to find my favorite dancing move.
The clock ticks away, laughing on the wall,
As I trip over joy, in this grand morning ball.

And as the sun sets, I promise to try,
To enjoy the mishaps, under the twilight sky.
With laughter and chaos, I'll toast to today,
For in life's little dance, there's magic at play.

Marks of Each Passing Moment

There's a sock in the fridge, does it chill or freeze?
I look for my glasses, still on my knees.
The dog steals my sandwich, he winks with a bark,
And I chuckle at nonsense, 'til it's way past dark.

The doorbell rings loud, 'tis the takeout parade,
They bring me my dinner, as confetti made.
I spill the sauce, like a modern art show,
And my napkin takes flight with a dramatic blow.

While I dance to tunes from the radio hum,
The dishes decide to play 'who'll be the dumb?'
I slip on some peas, my neighbors all stare,
As I twirl and I spin, without a single care.

In the kitchen, I weave the day into dreams,
With mishaps and laughter, flowing like streams.
Life's not a straight line, it's a zigzagged ride,
And with a pinch of humor, I wear chaos with pride.

Kindness Swirling in Routine

The toast pops up, a little too fast,
It leaps like a dancer, I'm sure it won't last.
The coffee spills over, an excited wave,
As I battle my morning with a grin, feeling brave.

The cat gives a yawn, as I look for my shoe,
While my breakfast debates if it's sticky or goo.
The squirrels in the yard, putting on a show,
Squeeing like mad, as they put on a row.

My neighbor waves over, while walking the cat,
Their pet wears a bowtie, looking fancy and fat.
He struts like a gentleman, with a lazy crunch,
While I munch my cereal, and raise my brunch.

With scrapes and squabbles, the day doesn't lack,
In the rhythm of life, I find joy in the crack.
So, wherever I wander, I'm sure to conjure,
A swirl of kindness, wrapped tight in laughter.

Life's Everlasting Whispers

The coffee pot sings, a melodious tune,
While my phone does a jig, like a neon balloon.
I cheat on my diet, while gathering spoons,
And my scales do a backflip, as time gently balloons.

The rain taps a rhythm, on the windowsill,
And I twirl with my socks, feeling such a thrill.
The cat wants to join in, meowing her cue,
While I guffaw at life, like it's all brand new.

The microwave beeps, like a robust friend,
Announcing desserts, like a playful trend.
With cake crumbs and giggles, I savor each bite,
As I laugh with my shadow, on this joyous night.

In the tapestry woven, of moments so sly,
There's magic in every misplaced French fry.
With a wink and a nudge, life whispers its charms,
In a world full of giggles, wrapped tight in warm arms.

Reflections in Routine's Mirror

Waking at dawn, the alarm's loud ring,
Grumbling like bears, we grumble and cling.
Coffee's a hero, it saves the day,
Mug in hand, we laugh and sway.

Toothpaste monster in mirror resides,
Brushing our teeth, the battle's implied.
Socks mismatched, but who really cares?
Life's little quirks hidden under our layers.

Lunch in a box with mystery meat,
Trade your banana for something sweet.
Cubicle mate has a joke to share,
Laughter erupts, it floats in the air.

At home, the cat gives an eye-roll glance,
Judging my dance in a solo prance.
Evening unfolds with a twist of fate,
Sleepyheads unite, but stay up too late.

Whispers of Morning Dew

Morning sunshine with a cheeky grin,
Sneaking through curtains, ready to win.
Grass wet with hope, I skip with glee,
Chasing squirrels, like they're chasing me.

Toast pops up, a buttery sight,
A dance of crumbs, oh what a delight.
Spill orange juice, a citrusy flood,
What's breakfast without a little food dud?

Neighbors chatting, their gossip is raw,
Dog barks loudly, breaking the law.
Pans start clattering, pots do a jig,
In this weird waltz, we all feel big.

Yet here we are with our daily grind,
Finding laughter in every kind.
Even the simplest things can keep,
Those giggles alive, no need to weep.

Simple Joys of Sunlight

Sunlight tickles the top of my head,
With shadows dancing, no need for bed.
Flip-flops flapping as I trot along,
Every step echoes a teasing song.

Children play tags with sunlight beams,
Chasing down clouds and their wild dreams.
Ice cream drips, oh what a mess,
Laughter erupts; I must confess.

Mowing the lawn, counting the stripes,
Get caught in a blur of buzzing gripes.
Grill smoke signals float up in the air,
Neighbors conniving with charred barbecue flair.

Evenings arrive with a twinkling wink,
The world spins softly, slow down to think.
Under the stars, we laugh like fools,
Celebrating life while breaking the rules.

Threads of Everyday Magic

Laundry piles high, a colorful sight,
Missing socks are now a fashion plight.
Tangled in sheets, a quest for the mate,
In the sock universe, twirls a new fate.

Dinner prep starts with a recipe lost,
Cooking calamities come at no cost.
Spices are sneaky, they jump in with flair,
A sprinkle of chaos, then kitchen despair.

TV time comes, remote on a quest,
On the couch we nest, our daily rest.
Show's a rerun, but laughs never cease,
In this routine, we find our peace.

Bedtime whispers, day swims to dream,
Let's toast to the quirks, life's silly theme.
Everyday moments hold a small spark,
Filling our hearts, even after dark.

Golden Glimmers in Routine

Oh look, my sock just made a run,
Unmatched, but oh so much fun!
The coffee spills, what a delight,
I greet the morn with a playful bite.

My cat's a ninja, moves so sly,
He leaps, he twirls, he'll surely fly!
The toast is burnt, what a surprise,
I'll eat it fast, with cheesy fries!

Each tiny mishap makes me grin,
Life's little laughs, where to begin?
Dancing forks, and spoons that sing,
Routine's a stage, let laughter ring!

So here's to blunders, big and small,
In our odd ballet, we have it all!
With silly moments nicely combined,
We paint our days with joy intertwined.

Unfurling the Commonplace

Woke up and stubbed my toe anew,
A morning greeting, how rude of you!
The cereal's dancing in its bowl,
With milk as a partner, loose control!

The dog threw his toy, bounced off the wall,
He's chasing shadows, that ninja ball!
Socks in the dryer, a missing mate,
In this great heist, who'll set the date?

Dinner's a mix, no recipe found,
A pinch of this, some chaos around.
The pasta's stuck, the sauce on the floor,
I think I've cooked up a tad too much lore!

So raise a glass to the everyday freaks,
To laughter, mishaps, and kitchen leaks.
In every moment, so dull or spry,
Life's winking at us, oh my, oh my!

Captured in Daily Breath

I went for a jog, but tripped on a leaf,
A fresh face plant, no time for grief!
The squirrels laughed, with nuts in their hands,
While I pondered how luck often stands!

Talked to my plant, oh what a delight,
It whispered back, "You're quite a sight!"
A neighbor's dog stole my unwatched shoe,
It's fashion now, didn't you know too?

Lunch was a mix of leftovers bizarre,
A taco, some sushi, dessert in a jar!
I bit into cake, thought it was cheese,
A culinary con, but it brought me ease!

So here's to the quirks in the daily grind,
Where joy isn't rare, it's entwined.
In each little joke, the universe plays,
Reminding us all that life's full of rays!

Essence of the Infinite Now

The noon sun dances on my messy hair,
While I search for my socks hiding somewhere.
Got stuck in a box, I couldn't find the way,
A hard hat required? I just might stay!

My fridge is a puzzle of leftovers there,
A fine gourmet feast, if you dare to compare!
The mixing bowls joined in a vibrant fight,
As I made a salad that took flight!

Traffic jam? Oh, sing a tune,
With honks and beeps, we'll all be in tune!
The world's a circus, and we're in the act,
With humor our glue, let's keep it intact!

So toast to the moments that don't quite fir,
With laughter as fuel, we'll go far, we're sure!
In this wacky show, where life takes a bow,
We find joy's pure essence, here and now!

Tapestry of Mundane Delight

In the morning, toast pops up,
Like a feathered bird on a cup.
Coffee drips a tune just right,
As I dance in my pajamas, quite the sight!

The mailman wears a superhero cape,
Dodging cats, he's a lively shape.
Grocery carts, a bumper car race,
As I search for snacks with a wild grace!

Neighbors wave, each with a grin,
While kids in chaos play akin.
A bicycle limping with a squeak,
Echoes laughter, oh what a week!

Evening rolls, and we declare,
Dinner's pizza, with flair to spare.
Every day a stage for fun,
A routine dance, oh what a run!

Canvas of Common Life

The sun sneezes, in a bright display,
As I fumble with my socks, hooray!
A bird does a jig on the window ledge,
Chasing dreams right off the edge!

Dust bunnies hold a dance-off race,
Under the couch, it's a lively place.
I trip on shoes left everywhere,
Like a circus clown, I'm quite the pair!

Afternoon comes with a blaring sound,
The blender's roar, like a lion unbound.
Spatula twirls, and the kitchen sings,
A chef in my mind, oh, the joy it brings!

Night invites stars in a waltzing spree,
As I argue with the TV (it's key).
Remote's missing, under the bed,
The daily antics swirl in my head!

Essence of Timeless Rituals

Morning wake-up calls come with a yawp,
Hair's a nest, resembling a mop.
Oatmeal spills like confetti bright,
As I juggle breakfast, oh, what a sight!

The dog fetches socks, not the ball,
A game of hide and seek in the hall.
Laundry monsters growl from the bin,
While I cheer the socks with a grin!

Work emails ping like a party tonight,
While I hide from my screen, out of sight.
A conference call with a cat's purr,
As they try to join in, what a stir!

Evening snuggles with a slice of pie,
Dreams of tomorrow, oh me, oh my!
Mundane moments, funny and bright,
Each day a treasure, what sheer delight!

Glimmers in the Gloaming

Under a sky painted with hues,
A squirrel mimics the evening blues.
I chase my keys, a lost little sprite,
While dusk gathers, a whimsical sight!

Neighbors laugh, kids play tag,
On my porch, I spill my brag.
A wordy gossip of plants and toast,
Celebrating the day, what I love most!

Dinner prep looks like a food fight,
As I juggle dishes, oh what a fright!
Spice jars ballet on the counter nice,
Every pinch, a dance, every taste, a slice!

Nightfall brings a comic book flair,
With superheroes in the air.
Each sleepy bedtime has its own jest,
In this colorful life, I am blessed!

Radiance of Daily Encounters

Morning light spills down like syrup,
A toast to the toast that's stuck in the slot.
Socks mismatched, a forgotten perk,
Life's little chaos, a daily plot.

Bumping into friends, what a delight,
With jokes and laughter, the hours soar.
Umbrellas flipped, what a sight,
Chasing puddles, who could ask for more?

Lost in the aisles of a grocery store,
Cart collisions sound like a horn.
We giggle as we reach for more,
The humor in shopping; we are reborn.

Evening falls, paintbrush strokes in pink,
Dinner spills as we clink our plates.
Finding joy in every wink,
Isn't life just a series of fates?

The Poetry of Simple Existence

Waking up to a cat's loud meow,
Coffee drips like a soothing song.
Slippers chase dust bunnies somehow,
Each morning mishap feels just so wrong.

The traffic light turns, but not my luck,
Cars dance around like they lost the thread.
I wave to a stranger, share the chuck,
Life spins round, a merry dread.

Lunchbox bites that taste like a trip,
Leftover pizza may steal the show.
In every bite, a little quip,
Food that smiles back, it's quite the glow.

The sun sets slow, shadows take stage,
A dance with time, in true cavalcade.
With every stumble, we write a page,
In the book of laughter, we are remade.

Gemstones in the Hourglass

Pebbles in my shoe bring a twinge,
Walking to work is a jolly game.
With every step, life starts to cring,
Those pesky stones always stake their claim.

Elevator stops like a dramatic show,
With strangers wrapped in their own world.
Eyes locked in awkward, face aglow,
Each silence sings, unfurled and swirled.

Coffee breaks filled with silly tales,
A spill that's a laugh, my shirt a canvas.
With laughter echoing like sweet gales,
In the mishap grows a true happiness.

Golden hour dips, laughter abounds,
Sharing stories like scattered seeds.
Joy blooms wild in the echoing sounds,
In the hourglass, every giggle leads.

Laughter in Coffee Sips

A line for coffee feels like a play,
Every sip a story, a twist in the plot.
The barista draws a frown, then a sway,
With cups raised high, we laugh a lot.

I spill my dreams on the tablecloth,
As crumbs bear witness, we roll our eyes.
Each sip echoes with a hearty froth,
In the café, joy is the prized surprise.

People-watching is a side delight,
As laughter bubbles like boiling tea.
A child's giggle takes glorious flight,
In every moment, wild glee runs free.

Evening coffee, the saga ignites,
With friends around, the cheer multiplies.
Share a laugh 'til the moonlight bites,
Every sip's a secret, where glee never dies.

The Poetry of Presence

Waking up with bedhead flair,
Coffee spills like liquid air.
Socks that never match in style,
Yet here I smile, yes, here I smile.

Cats plotting world domination,
Chasing dust, what a sensation!
The phone rings and it's just a spam,
Life's little quirks, like a grand slam.

Dancing with a broom in hand,
Stumbling like a one-man band.
Neighbors peek with puzzled looks,
Life's a joke, and laughter cooks.

Oh, the bliss of mundane bliss,
Each silly moment can't be missed.
Turning chores into a play,
Every flub makes brighter day.

Celebrating Quiet Journeys

Waking up to find my shoes,
Misplaced again, what can I use?
Coffee brewed, but tastes like mud,
Oops, my day is off with a thud.

Walking out, and it starts to rain,
Just my luck, oh what a gain!
Umbrella snapped, a real delight,
Raindrops dance—such a silly sight.

Strangers smile, their faces bright,
Sharing jokes while waiting in light.
The bus arrives, a circus ride,
Holding tight, I laugh inside.

Finding magic in daily fuss,
Little hiccups turn to plus.
Every footstep, every turn,
In humor's light, the world does burn.

Captivity in Comfort

Pajamas snug, a fortress grand,
Couch is king, remote in hand.
Snacks in tow, I'm never late,
Culinary skills? Observe my plate.

Binge-watching shows, what a spree,
Who needs plans? Just you and me!
Takeout menus, our daily spread,
Living luxury in crumbs instead.

Pets as landlords, oh so sly,
Guarding seats, as they pass by.
Snoozing sounds like TV's hum,
Cozy chaos, is it a conundrum?

Perhaps this couch could get a throne,
Ruling comfort, my happy zone.
In this bliss, I'm stuck for good,
Contemplating snacks, as one should.

Unfolding of Yesterday's Dreams

Old postcards from a distant place,
Scribbled notes that time can't erase.
Doodles in the margins clear,
A comedy of youth, my dear.

Once a dream of flying high,
Now I trip while passing by.
The world's a stage, in my pajamas,
Each little blunder, fitting dramas.

Past adventures cheerfully blend,
Every oops, a heartfelt friend.
Laughter echoes with each recall,
Memory's stage, I hear the call.

As new dreams take a playful wing,
Dancing through life's silly fling.
Each giggle and snort, we redeem,
In the unfolding of yesterday's dream.

Songs from the Heart of Home

In the kitchen, pots start to dance,
With spoons as their partners, in a bubbly trance.
The coffee pot whistles a cheeky tune,
While toast pops up like a warm balloon.

A cat in a box plays hide and seek,
While kids draw mustaches on Dad's old cheek.
The plants chime in with a leafy sway,
As laundry sings songs of the clothesline play.

The fridge hums a melody, cool and bright,
As leftovers argue what's wrong or right.
It's a circus of laughter, a mishap parade,
In the heart of our home, where memories are made.

Even the clock ticks with a wicked grin,
Counting the moments where chaos begins.
So here's to the laughter, the tickle and tease,
In our charming abode, we're never uneased.

Traces of Light in the Shadows

The shadows stretch long when the sun says goodbye,
But mystery dances with a wink in the sky.
With giggles of owls and crickets' delight,
It's a playful night under the moon's soft light.

We chase silly shadows on the living room wall,
Pretending to be giants, so grand and so tall.
The dog thinks we're nuts, he barks in surprise,
As the family all giggles and crashes like fries.

Footsteps echo with whispers of glee,
As we venture through hallways, wild and free.
The pantry holds secrets, well-hidden and sweet,
For snacks turn into treasures we eagerly meet.

So let's dance in the dark, with our silly old grins,
For the traces of light bring out our wild spins.
In the end, it's the laughter that steals the night,
As the moon holds our secrets, so calm and so bright.

Wonder in Each Sunrise's Gaze

The rooster crows loudly to welcome the dawn,
While sleepy-eyed humans all yawn and fawn.
With coffee in hand, we blink at the sky,
As squirrels play tag, oh my, oh my!

Birds chirp their tunes, a delightful surprise,
While the sun stretches out, yawning wide with its rise.
The toast starts to dance in the warm, little pan,
As breakfast declares, it has a grand plan!

Mismatched socks wander, seeking their mates,
While the dog tries to catch what he thinks are old plates.
In a world full of wonder, each sunrise brings cheer,
With giggles and mischief, it's plain and it's clear.

With every new morning, we laugh at the day,
For the wonder in life is just games that we play.
So let's embrace the daylight, with all of its quirks,
As we celebrate mornings with all of their perks!

Neat Little Packages of Joy

With boxes all wrapped, and ribbons galore,
Each corner we peek brings surprises in store.
The cat claims the paper as her cozy new bed,
While the kids laugh and giggle, "Hey, that's my head!"

From toys to sweet treats, what's tucked in each case?
A delightful adventure, a hide-and-seek race.
With laughter exploding, as bows start to fly,
In a whirlwind of chaos, the fun's standing high.

We search through the gifts, finding treasures untold,
A rubber chicken, some stickers, and gum that is gold.
With each twist of a ribbon, and shine in our eyes,
We unwrap all the pleasures of laughter and sighs.

So here's to the moments in shiny disguise,
In neat little packages, where joy always lies.
Where love fills the air, and silliness reigns,
For happiness found is a joy that remains.

Whirlwinds of Ordinary Affection

In the morning, socks take flight,
Chasing the cat in pure delight.
Coffee spills, a splashy show,
Who needs a circus? Just watch us glow.

The neighbors dance, a crazy sight,
Waving like they're in a fight.
Birds gossip loud, the gossip's clear,
Even the mailman is full of cheer.

Left my keys in the fridge last night,
Pancakes flipped with unearned might.
Laundry's a puzzle, socks wander bold,
Remnants of chaos, colorful and old.

So here's to life, in all its mess,
A tumble of laughter, we're truly blessed.
In every blunder, love finds a way,
Each day spins magic, come what may.

Softness of Evening's Glow

The sun dips low, a golden tease,
Neighbors swap stories, sipping on freeze.
A cat perched high on a fence of wood,
Unbothered, he reigns, as every cat should.

Children chase bubbles that float by fast,
With giggles and shrieks, a joy unsurpassed.
Dinner burns slightly, smoke wafts around,
Not all of our meals are perfectly browned.

Streetlights flicker, a dance of their own,
Casting strange shadows where laughter has grown.
An ice cream truck's jingle fills the air,
For a moment, we forget every care.

Under the stars, laughter pops like corn,
Here in this chaos, new dreams are born.
We toast to the silly, the quirk of the night,
In the wake of giggles, everything's right.

Illuminating the Unseen

The morning sun spills like syrup sweet,
Cereal dances, a crunchy beat.
Toast jumps up, the butter flies,
Breakfast is served with a side of spies.

Lawnmowers roar, a musical fuss,
Trying to tame nature, it's quite the bus.
A squirrel steals snacks right from our hand,
While we laugh at his bold little stand.

Puddles reflect the blue skies above,
Splashing around, it's all about love.
Neighbors are sharing their funny old tales,
Of lost shoes and mail from faraway trails.

As twilight whispers, fireflies blink,
While we sip lemonade and stop to think.
Life's little quirks, the gleam in our eyes,
Bring warmth and joy 'neath those vast, starry skies.

Glimpses of Everyday Splendor

Every lilac bloom's a whimsical dance,
Bees buzzing loudly, sipping romance.
Insects buzzing, a comic parade,
Life's little moments are not to fade.

Laundry hangs like an art exhibit,
Colors mismatched, a bold little visit.
Wind chimes giggle, they know the score,
Laughing at pigeons who claim to soar.

Stumbling upon a friend in the store,
Where toothpaste and snacks lead to tales galore.
In the mundane, funny finds its place,
A monkey wrench grin on each shopper's face.

So lift up your eyes, let laughter unfold,
In rhythms of life, pure stories are told.
Together we wander through simple delight,
Finding each twist in the shimmering light.

The Quiet Magic of Here and Now

A sock that's lost its way, we find,
In depths of cushions, quite aligned.
It waves at us with cheeky flair,
A little joy that's hiding there.

A cat that leaps, a coffee spill,
Each moment brings a tiny thrill.
With laughter echoing around,
In silly chaos, joy is found.

The clock ticks slow, we sip away,
At life that dances, here to stay.
A sandwich flipped, the dog does prance,
In daily quirks, we find our chance.

The sun sets low, the moon on high,
We giggle softly, passersby.
Silly moments, fleeting fast,
The magic's here, we'll make it last.

Fleeting Feathers of Hope

A feather drops, a bird's delight,
It tickles noses, takes to flight.
In windy whispers, dreams will tease,
We chase them down with silly ease.

A puddle forms, we make a splash,
Like little kids, in a wild dash.
With goofy grins and laughter loud,
We're superheroes, chasing clouds.

The clouds then gather, rain does fall,
We dance in joy, we heed its call.
With each drip drop, a giggle's born,
In silly storms, we're never torn.

And when the sun breaks through the gray,
We wave goodbye to disarray.
A smile shared, the world feels wide,
In fleeting feathers, we abide.

Glories in a Cup of Tea

The kettle sings a merry tune,
A dance of steam beneath the moon.
We spill the leaves, oh, what a mess,
In fragrant chaos, we find finesse.

A biscuit crumbles in our hands,
We laugh out loud, forget our plans.
With sugar cubes, like tiny rocks,
We cheer for joy in all the flocks.

Each sip reveals a tale to share,
Of sassy spoons and cozy chairs.
In porcelain palaces, we reign,
With giggles rising like the steam.

Neighbors peer in, they shake their heads,
At tea time mischief, tales in threads.
Yet in this warmth, we weave our dreams,
In glories found, life truly beams.

The Serenity of Returning Home

A door swings wide, a cat does glare,
She claims her throne, beyond compare.
With every step, we hear a song,
In cozy corners, we belong.

A sock on stairs, a book misplaced,
Each little laugh, we hug and chase.
From kitchen scents and scattered shoes,
In our own rhythm, we can't lose.

The fridge hums soft, a dance we know,
With snacks that greet us, oh, what a show!
We toast to life with silly cheers,
In every corner, love appears.

With sunset glow, we settle down,
In our sweet haven, never frown.
Each hug, each sigh, a gentle dome,
The world feels light when we're at home.

Threads of Everyday Magic

A sock that dances on the floor,
It mischiefs whispers, begs for more.
Tea cups giggle, cookies tease,
Laughter hides behind the cheese.

A tangle of dreams in morning light,
Juggling eggs feels just so right.
Spilled paint looks like modern art,
Every blunder plays its part.

The cat steals hearts, and half my seat,
Bouncing around, oh what a feat!
Chairs that swear they can't stand still,
Who knew boredom had such skill?

A pie in the sky, or was it a bird?
Mundane magic, you've heard the word!
Life's a circus, don't take a bow,
Take a selfie with the cow!

Sunlight on Familiar Paths

A squirrel with shades on, looking cool,
Steals my lunch – breaking all the rules!
The garden gnomes are plotting schemes,
They have their meetings, or so it seems.

Puddles reflect my rainy grin,
With every splash, I dip and spin.
The streetlights flicker, dance in line,
Twirling like they've had some wine!

A fly that buzzes, thinks he's smart,
Imploding dreams, tearing apart.
But hey! That's just the way it goes,
In a world where anything glows.

Each day's a riddle wrapped in fun,
From the rising moon to setting sun.
Hold my coffee as I twirl,
In the sunlight's hug, let's swirl!

Enchantment of the Unremarkable

A chair with crumbs that tells a tale,
Of midnight snacks and a few pails.
Paperclips whisper secrets low,
While toasters get jealous of the dough.

The carpet feels the weight of dreams,
As I trip over it – or so it seems.
The clock ticks loud, and then it's shy,
Counts the seconds as they fly.

Laundry piles sing a haughty tune,
Wearing socks that clash with the moon!
Spaghetti's fighting with a fork,
Every bite a joyous quirk!

The pen rolls off, claims it's not a child,
While papers shuffle, poorly filed.
In every mishap, there's delight,
Who knew the mundane could take flight?

Songs of the Silent Hours

The fridge hums softly, a late-night tune,
Underneath the watchful moon.
Crumbs talk back from the pantry door,
Where yesterday's dinner becomes folklore.

The bathroom mirror shrieks out a joke,
While I'm brushing my teeth in smoke.
Bathtubs sing when the bubbles rise,
And rubber ducks have secret pies.

Midnight snacks sneak in on their toes,
Pretzel whispers nobody knows.
The alarm clock snoozes, takes a dive,
In dreams where silly critters thrive.

A dance party starts in the quiet breeze,
Dust bunnies prancing with utmost ease.
Oh, how the hours twist and play,
In the quiet chaos of a normal day!

The Light in Each Ordinary Hour

In the midst of cereal spills,
Laughter dances in the air.
A cat's leap over morning thrills,
Makes breakfast a comical affair.

With socks that never quite match,
We stumble through our sleepy days.
Like a dog's bark in a snappy patch,
Life's chaos in the funniest ways.

Umbrellas upside down in rain,
Chasing puddles, oh what a sight!
Like a clown car on a serpentine train,
Each twist brings joy, pure delight.

So here's to the quirks we embrace,
Every mishap, a chuckling sound.
In daily madness, we find our place,
With giggles where laughter is found.

Reflections on a Quiet Lane

Strolling down the path I know,
A squirrel steals the last of my snack.
In rhythm with the breeze's flow,
I chuckle at the sneaky hack.

The neighbor's dog, a furry knight,
Guards the mailbox with great pride.
But one swift bark, oh, what a fright,
Turns my stroll into a wild ride!

Pigeons strut like they've got style,
Waddling with a hip-hop sway.
They pause, then fly, all the while,
Claiming the sidewalk's runway.

In the whisper of a gentle breeze,
Life parades its funny quests.
Each step we take, a laugh to seize,
In these small moments, joy rests.

Delights Found in Everyday Chatter

At the café, with coffee in hand,
Conversations bubble like a brew.
Stories fly like a marching band,
Each sip brings something new to chew.

The barista's jokes, a daily treat,
As spills and laughs mix in the air.
A mix-up that can't be beat,
Turns a latte into a flair!

With friends retelling tales so wild,
We laugh till we can't breathe at all.
Each punchline, like a playful child,
Brings joy that can't help but sprawl!

In every laugh and silly quirk,
Life's simple joys we can't forget.
Daily banter, like a playful perk,
Leaves us grinning without regret.

Embraces of Gentle Rituals

Waking up, the alarm's a tease,
Header socks now lost in space.
Coffee spills with such great ease,
Morning adventures start the race.

The yoga mat, a tangled mess,
Fall over and let out a laugh.
Strikes a pose, but no success,
Turns into a wobbly giraffe.

While dinner's cooking, pots in sync,
A dance-off with the high-pitched tunes.
Some mishap there leads to a wink,
Much to the delight of our spoons.

So here's to rituals so sweet,
Each moment wrapped in fun divine.
In all the chaos, we find our beat,
Life's a stage, let joy be the sign.

Echoes of Laughter in Stillness

A cat in a hat steals a chair,
While I trip on my socks in despair.
The toast jumps up, it's quite a sight,
In the morning chaos, everything's right.

The dog barks loudly, thinking he's smart,
Chasing his tail, oh what a start!
As coffee spills down my favorite shirt,
I can't help but laugh at my daily flirt.

The neighbors all peek through their blinds,
Wondering what joy in laughter finds.
With pancake faces and syrup spread,
Living this life makes it fun, I said!

Vibrant socks dance in the sun,
Who knew laundry could be so much fun?
Each moment a giggle, a stampede of cheer,
In this silly ballet, I've nothing to fear.

Melodies of Routine Heartbeats

Alarm clocks sing their loud, shrill tune,
While I stumble like a sleepy raccoon.
Breakfast with cereal flying around,
Who needs a circus when chaos is found?

Brush in one hand, and a shoe in the other,
I prepare for the day like a well-fed smother.
With toothpaste on lips that stretch in surprise,
I sparkle with laughter, a jester in disguise.

From work to the play and back to the grind,
I juggle my tasks with humor aligned.
Meetings in suits can be quite a joke,
While I play the role of a caffeinated bloke.

Evening brings sitcoms with laughter galore,
Cracking up over life and its uproar.
The mundane becomes a riotous show,
With every heartbeat, the warmth grows.

Subtle Sparks in Each Breath

A sneeze turns into a giggle parade,
As I chase my sneaky cat with a spade.
The mailman waves, his hat askew,
Wondering if my bouquet has grown too.

Each honk from traffic feels like a cheer,
Where chaos and laughter blend, oh dear!
The sun plays peekaboo through the trees,
While I dance with the leaves in the gentle breeze.

Dinner's a comedy of pots and pans,
As spaghetti slips away from my hands.
With smiles in the kitchen, we stir up the night,
Creating a feast that just feels so right.

As stories unfold over dessert and tea,
Life's little moments feel wildly free.
We giggle at mishaps, let out a cheer,
Celebrating the sparkles in every sphere.

Flickers of Warmth and Wonder

Morning light streams through the window bright,
I trip over slippers with morning delight.
Toast pops up like a surprise in the air,
Butter smiles down with a comforting flair.

In the park as kids race, oh what a scene,
Running like they're part of a cartoon machine.
I join in their laughter, can't help but jump,
Falling in sync with the giggles and thump.

Even when skies make a frowning face,
I twirl in puddles, a silly embrace.
The world may feel heavy, but laughter is light,
Dancing through storms, we take on the night.

At day's end, with stars shining bright,
We share tales of wonder, with all hearts alight.
Life's quirky adventures, woven in jest,
Together, we find that we're truly blessed.

Puzzles of Enjoyable Routine

Morning coffee spills, what a sight,
The cat looks at me, ready to fight.
Toast pops up, looking a little burnt,
I cheerfully laugh, amid the day's turnt.

Socks mismatched, a fashion faux pas,
Dance with my dog, flapping his paw.
Chasing my keys, that old daily game,
Yet each silly stumble, I can't help but claim.

Lunchbox treasures, who thought of this?
A cookie surprise? Oh, what pure bliss!
Fruits in a frenzy, rolling away,
A snack time scuffle, but hey, that's my day!

Evenings end with a jumbled book,
Page 10 and then back, let's take a look.
Laughter erupts in blurry delight,
As my quirks shine through in the fading light.

Journey through Ordinary Gyres

Alarm clock blares, it's that time again,
Slippers in hand, my best buddy's my pen.
Breakfast chaos, cereal on the floor,
Nothing quite says 'fun' like a toaster war!

Outfit choices, a circus of hues,
Wearing my shirt, with last night's stew views.
Muffled giggles as the door shuts tight,
Watch for those squirrels—what a comical sight!

Traffic jams transform into dance-offs bright,
No rhythm in me, but what a delight!
Strangers glance over, sharing a grin,
As I bust a move, 'neath the jazz of the din.

Evening brings laughter, the best kind of tease,
Dinnertime chat, stories that please.
With mishaps and giggles that never will fade,
In life's little moments, joy's surely made.

Momentary Havens in Busy Lives

A coffee break feels like a grand tour,
That donut I snatched, oh, who could ignore?
Jumps of joy when the good news arrives,
How can I savor? Oh, the fun thrives!

Tripping on steps like it's all in the plan,
Fall into laughter with my best friend Stan.
Gathering stories from every small pause,
Life's in the moments, the laughter, the cause!

Meetings that drift into dizzying dreams,
Like a circus of whispers, floating on beams.
'Let's brainstorm!' they say, as my mind starts to stray,
Until I'm back giggling, passing the day.

End of the day brings a soft-hearted cheer,
Chasing our tales, that's what we hold dear.
In blunders and giggles, our spirits unwind,
Finding true joy just by being kind.

Smiles Shared with Familiar Faces

Morning smiles, they light up the room,
Neighbors exchanging their tales of doom.
Laundry on lines like banners of cheer,
Colorful socks flying, oh dear, oh dear!

Bumping the cart in the grocery aisle,
Laughing at prices that make us all smile.
Stories of lattes that splattered on dress,
In moments of chaos, we're far from a mess.

Playground antics, sliced apples askew,
Children giggling at the skies' brilliant hue.
Watch them all chase bubbles up high,
And we can't help but laugh with a sigh.

As day turns to dusk, goodness alights,
Sharing our stories under soft city lights.
With laughter resounding and love filling space,
In this comical journey, we all find our place.

Caress of the Soft Wind

The breeze tickles my nose,
As the squirrels play tag, I suppose.
Clouds float by without a care,
While I hop like a jellybean in midair.

Sunshine sneaks through the trees,
I do a little dance, just to please.
The flowers giggle, swaying so spry,
Wondering why I'm waving goodbye.

Birds gossip in the fluffy sky,
I join their chat, oh me, oh my!
With every whisper of sweet air,
I'm convinced I've got not a worry to share.

Laughter tumbles from above,
Nature knows just what I love.
Every gust brings a silly grin,
In this playful world, how can I not win?

Stories Spoken in Silence

The clocks tick softly, like a sigh,
While coffee spills, oh me, oh my!
A creaky chair has tales to tell,
If only my muffin would stop its swell.

Cats stretch and curl, with such finesse,
On windowsills, they look like a mess.
Their silent meows call out to dreams,
While I laugh at my cereal's quirky beams.

A book waits patient on the shelf,
It rolls its eyes, like it's judging myself.
With every page, the world spins round,
In silence, life's mysteries abound.

The moon winks down, a cheeky spark,
In shadows, I find a dancing lark.
Each pause whispers secrets to the night,
In the stillness, I twinkle with delight.

Celebrations of Daily Moments

Morning toast does a little jig,
As butter glides, oh what a gig!
Eggs bounce proudly on their plates,
In this breakfast ball, who knows their fates?

A stroll brings bells and whirly tunes,
With every step, I dance with the dunes.
Sidewalk chalk raves, all colors bright,
Drawing hopscotch, oh what a sight!

Lunch is a party, complete with flair,
The salad twirls, with vinaigrette hair.
Cookies giggle in their sweet array,
As I snag a bite and shout hooray!

The sun dips low with a bow so grand,
While the stars burst forth, a glittering band.
Each moment's a gift, wrapped up with cheer,
In the wild celebration of being here!

Shimmers of Life's Simple Joys

A raindrop dances on my cheek,
With each little splash, I feel unique.
Puddles reflect a silly spree,
I jump right in, who cares, just me!

Sandcastles rise with sandy might,
As waves giggle, asking for a fight.
Seagulls squawk, they join the play,
While I wave at all and say, 'Hooray!'

A simple smile from a stranger's face,
Turns the world into a joyous place.
Lollipop stick stuck to my shoe,
I waddle along, feeling brand new.

Hearts twinkle under a starry embrace,
With twinkling laughter, we fill the space.
Life sparkles in its humorous way,
In the shimmers we find, let's dive and sway!

Notes from an Unwritten Day

Awake with socks mismatched and bright,
Coffee spills like morning light.
Birds chirp gossip in the trees,
While I chase crumbs of yesterday's cheese.

Spilled cereal, a crunchy tune,
A dance with a cat under the moon.
Outfits chosen, yet wildly askew,
Who cares when the sun greets you?

Neighbors wave with a puzzled grin,
As I wave back, forgetting my chin.
Laughter bubbles in twinkling streams,
Turns out the world is stitched from dreams.

Naps pop up, a surprise delight,
Pajama parties every night.
Tomorrow's worries take a break,
As we savor the flake of a cake.

Petals of Routine Blossoms

The toaster sings a morning song,
While toast leaps out, just to prolong.
I chase it down like a hungry knight,
Who knew breakfast could start a fight?

The clock's hands dance a jaunty jig,
Pants are worn like a stubborn twig.
With socks that squeak on hardwood floor,
I slide right out the kitchen door.

My to-do list somehow got lost,
Coffee? It's worth the utmost cost.
A squirrel mocks me from a branch,
Oh, could today just take a chance?

As routine blossoms, petals fall,
Each giggle answering the call.
Life's quirks weave stories yet untold,
In the garden of joy, we grow bold.

Embrace of a Sunset's Smile

The sun bends low with a wink so grand,
As shadows dance, a jolly band.
Ice cream drips, a sticky mess,
Laughter erupts, we couldn't care less.

Clouds flip-flop in a vibrant display,
While we giggle in a silly ballet.
A dog chases laughter through the park,
Stealing hearts as the sun starts to spark.

The day wraps up with a sleepy yawn,
But not before we mispaint the dawn.
Colors bleed like a toddler's art,
In the hug of evening, we play our part.

With fireflies twinkling their tiny light,
We find magic in the falling night.
The sunset smiles, a grand delight,
Tomorrow's blunders are sure to excite.

Chasing the Subtle Spark

A banana peel, a slip, whoa there!
Life decides to play a funny dare.
I bounce back with an epic laugh,
Witness this comedy, a lil' gaffe.

The wind whispers secrets, what a tease,
I chase after jokes carried with ease.
A paper plane takes flight with style,
Each ruffled page, a reason to smile.

Dandelions bobble like tiny clowns,
As I prance about in mismatched gowns.
Every step is a turn as I hop,
To chase the spark, I never stop.

The evening wraps with giggly sighs,
Underneath a blanket of starry skies.
Chasing whimsy, we gleefully roam,
In the heart of laughter, we find our home.

www.ingramcontent.com/pod-product-compliance
Lightning Source LLC
Chambersburg PA
CBHW062112280426
43661CB00086B/494

9781805860860